THE MADNESS OF CHEFS
NEW AND SELECTED POEMS

Other books by Elaine Magarrell:

On Hogback Mountain
Blameless Lives
Inventory

The Madness of Chefs

NEW AND SELECTED POEMS

by

Elaine Magarrell

Edited by Barbara Goldberg
Catherine Harnett
& Jean Nordhaus

THE WORD WORKS
Washington, D.C.

FIRST EDITION
Copyright © 2017 Debra Conklin

Reproduction of any part of this book in any form or by any means, electronic or mechanical, except when quoted in part for the purpose of review, must have written permission from the publisher. Address all such inquiries to us at:
The Word Works P.O. Box 42164
Washington, D.C., 20015 or at
editor@wordworksbooks.org.

Cover design: Susan Pearce Design.
Author Photograph: Jeffrey Conklin.

ISBN: 978-1-944585-15-0
LCCN: 2016963761

Acknowledgments

Some of this work appeared in journals, texts, and anthologies, sometimes in slightly altered versions.

Bedford Introduction to Literature; *Bedford Introduction to Poetry*; *Hadoar*; *Hungry As We Are*; *Innisfree*; *Jewish Women's Literary Annual (Volume 7, 2006)*; *Light Year*; *Lip Service*; *Mediphores*; *Passager*; *Poet Lore*; *Potomac Review*; *Ruby*; *Shirim*; *The Takoma Voice*; *The Wolf Head Quarterly*; *Yankee*; and the WPFW-FM Poetry Anthology: "The First 300 Poets on 'The Poet and the Poem.'"

THE WORD WORKS
is grateful for the poetry of Elaine Magarrell
and the generous support
of the Conklin / Magarrell family.

❧

Contents

FOREWORD ... 11

New Poems

The Madness of Chefs ... 17
Five Mortalities ... 18
The Joy of Cooking ... 19
You Are What You Eat ... 20
Appetite ... 21
Religion ... 22
One Day Soon ... 23
A Hard Piece on a Good Piano ... 25
September in Bar Harbor ... 26
Love and Other Burdens ... 27
Falling Apart ... 28
In Which We Limit Ourselves ... 29
A Life ... 30
Tundra Swans ... 31
Curiosity ... 32
Ecstasy ... 33
Aspects ... 34
The White Bird ... 35
Particulars ... 36
Looking Up from the Garden ... 37
The Possum ... 39
The Body's Needs ... 40
The Reluctant Optimist ... 41
The Long and Varied Lives of Breasts ... 42
Inheritance ... 43
The Lover ... 44
Motel ... 46
Tequila Sunrise ... 47

Local Anesthetic ... 48
There is a rumor ... 49
Circles ... 50
Sophie's Face ... 51
The Straw House ... 52
In My Element ... 53
Crone in Bloom ... 54
Psalm of the Outcast Jew ... 55
Dictionary of Occupations ... 56
Late for Death ... 57
My Haircutter Goes on Vacation ... 58
Rain from a Cloudless Sky ... 59
Charm School ... 60
Snow and Circumstance ... 61
What Mattered Then ... 63
Long Marriage ... 64
Jack Was Going Out the Door ... 65
The Bird Book ... 66
The Sweet Comfort of Denial ... 68
The Ingenuity of the Damned ... 70
The Good Lord Sees a Shrink ... 71
Haircut ... 73
Superwoman ... 74
My Mother, If She Had Won Free Dance Lessons ... 75
My Mother Couldn't Breathe ... 76
Lost ... 77
Good Things ... 78
Falling in Love ... 79
Knowing What Jack Gilbert Knew ... 80
Poetry in Bulgaria ... 81
What Deer Will Eat ... 82
The Young ... 83
The Limp ... 84
The Unfinished Poem ... 85
In the Mirror ... 86

Babel Reunion ... 87
The Cry ... 88
Leah Complains to God ... 90
Fragile ... 91
Greatness and Despair in the Arrangement of Words ... 92

From On Hogback Mountain (1985)

The Mother in Line 28 ... 95
The Truth About Bears ... 96
Mrs. Venture Advances ... 97
Mrs. Venture Does the Two-Step ... 98
Mrs. Venture Deals with Crime ... 99
Mrs. Venture Buys Time at a Health Club ... 100
Good Girl ... 101
Letter Home ... 102
Galesburg ... 103
Clinton 1942 ... 106
Zolana ... 107
Death ... 108
On Hogback Mountain ... 109
Wet ... 110
Rodeo ... 111
Refusing the Eye ... 112
Last Child ... 113
Words Have Sex Lives of Their Own ... 115

From Blameless Lives (1992)

Reunion ... 119
Somehow ... 121
Chickens ... 122

Zambia. Zimbabwe. On the Border ... 124
The Brain on Its Own ... 125
A Surfeit of Desire ... 126
Wings ... 127
Promise ... 128
Swimming ... 129
Odd ... 131
Advice ... 132
Entertaining Edelman; Ignoring Freud ... 133
Going So Far ... 134

From Inventory (2008)

Where the Blue Begins ... 137
The Day of Death ... 138
Channel Island Trail ... 139
The Peach of Immortality ... 140
Surprise Is Dying ... 141
Quantum Stuff ... 142

About the Author / About the Artist ... 145
About the Editors ... 146
Other Word Works Books ... 147

Foreword

Elaine Magarrell did not look the part of a poet. She was modest, unassuming and constitutionally unable to promote herself. She didn't go to writer conferences, didn't network. Thus, she never received the acclaim she deserved—and would've been so uncomfortable with. But when you read her poems, you cannot help but be struck by how fresh and original they are. Just read "Words Have Sex Lives of Their Own, or "Five Mortalities" or "The Joy of Cooking." Elaine doesn't write about life's storms, but rather time's ripples, punctuated by delicious food.

Once I asked Elaine what she would want for her last meal. "A perfectly ripe anjou pear, a piece of camembert and a glass of white wine," she replied. You'd think her poetry would be very refined—but it isn't. It's earthy, sometimes bawdy, the natural world presented without sentimentality, but with imagery so vivid it will take your breath away. In "The Long and Varied Lives of Breasts" she writes, "So docile they lay / like laughing girls in petticoats...."

Hers was a "leaping" mind—intuitive, free from the constraints of reason, free to fly with apparently little effort. Yet her poems are also infused with plain speech, Zen-like in their purity: "Sleep. I never tire of it." And on the day of death: "you won't have to meet / anyone new. You'll already / know everyone you love."

For more than thirty years, our small poetry group met at Elaine's and broke bread together, food she cooked and served with love. The meal was foreplay. The main course was intense critique of works in progress that went way beyond line edits.

Criticism isn't about right or wrong. It's about what one can digest. We had history, knew each other's true voice. We knew the world from whence the poems came. Our focus was on locating the poem's essence, what was necessary, what extraneous, and what was missing. Our discussions helped steer us toward what we meant to say, though we hadn't said it yet—or even thought it. And for Elaine's insights and nourishing spirit, I will always be grateful.

Barbara Goldberg
Chevy Chase, MD

I will not let her go.

She is sitting in her chair in the sunny room at the end, baffled by the T.V. and the cordless phone. I am of no help. I read her the Post, some poetry from random books. From her book, *Blameless Lives*. She is impressed with her talent. Elaine falls asleep, and I wonder if this will be the last visit.

For years, we were bound to each other through poetry. She and Barbara and I met twice a month to critique each other's work over dinner. Jack put on his hat, went to Spanish class, considerate. So many poems in this collection were on the menu. Her work took me into the quirky world where Mrs. Venture lived, where food was delicious, where squirrels and birds appeared and disappeared into the kingdom of loss. Elaine's poems are deceptively simple, but are wise and complex things. She had a unique way of taking the tiny and finding the big, and reducing the big into a tiny detail, the way a heron stands, or the taste of key lime pie.

The Madness of Chefs is an apt title. Elaine's poems are full of food: crispy chicken skin, raisin cake, oranges and apples, and of course, her sister's tongue and brother's dry heart.

And there is Elaine's version of time: there is the past where her parents make appearances, her mother dancing, her father laughing at his own jokes. The present has Jack, her children, strange animals in the yard, the coming and going of seasons. Elaine meets the future with equanimity, observing nature's cyclical comings and goings.

One of my indelible memories is of spending New Year's Eve with Jack and Elaine, Barbara and Moshe. We had dinner at Old Europe: Wiener Schnitzel and beets. A blind pianist with Shirley Temple curls sang Lily Marlene. Within one evening, we experienced time's cycle—old songs, a present spent among friends, the New Year arriving on time.

Her number will stay in my phone, her poetry in my bookcase, her beauty in my mind.

Catherine Harnett
Reston, VA

The Book of Proverbs tells us that the worth of a woman of valor is above jewels, and what can be more precious than a loyal, completely honest friend—especially if she's a fellow-poet and you share with one another your work-in-progress. Although I'd known Elaine tangentially, I got to know her well after I became president of Washington Writers' Publishing House, the cooperative poetry press that had published her first book, *On Hogback Mountain*. The aspect of my new position that most terrified me was fund-raising. Elaine stepped up to help and proceeded brilliantly, setting up meetings with foundation officers to shape proposals, writing grants, and raising the funds we needed to produce our next set of books. I'd had no idea.

This woman, seemingly so diffident, was astonishingly able. Our association developed into a friendship and sharing of poems that did not end until her death.

Elaine could not lie. "I will be a good girl," she wrote, "smile until my mouth aches. / I will not tell the truth. / I will not tell the truth." Her intelligence and character were such that she could not engage in the usual diplomatic platitudes and evasions that for most people soothe and lubricate the rough edges of their interactions with others. This quality often made it difficult for her navigating in the social and po-biz worlds, but it made her a spot-on critic and a superb poet. I could never be happy with a poem unless I knew it had passed Elaine's muster; she had a sure instinct for the soft spot, for inflation, all forms of puffery, the false move. She could not lie, but she could leap, and her poems, full of wild humor, imagination, and acute perception, are touched with that higher madness that makes for sublimest sanity.

I miss her presence in this world, but treasure these poems that hold the best of her brilliant, intuitive spirit.

Jean Nordhaus
Washington, D.C.

New Poems

The Madness of Chefs

Let us now praise the madness of chefs, their exaltation
in searing heat, their need for murder, desire for stress.
How they perform with the delicate, even sublime, fingering
blood and blossom and bean. How they scatter
the sacred herbs, distill the sea to fish and salt, the sky above
to yeast and bird. They conserve the fresh-killed rabbit,
salvaging even its scream in their night, preserving its offal
and tripe. They cooked the last supper for Jesus,
made cakes for Marie Antoinette, fixed a final meal
for the murderer, fed Caesar and Cleo in bed. They plate
foie gras for the eyes but hope for it to be laid waste. Awash
with wine. The taste. The taste. Heavenly vapors
invade the nose. What a long way they've come since they first
scorched meat. Since the caveman fed his spitting fire.
And as fuel is shoved into the gut, what a catharsis,
belly at peace, what a fullness of spirit and at the end,
a busy bowel dealing spotlessly with excrement. Let us
all praise the madness of chefs. Come to the table
beggars and queens. They're at it again.

Five Mortalities

Five mortalities sat in the dining room feasting
on shrimp. Five deaths to be finishing off
the bread pudding and exchanging photographs.
None made any noise when the hot coffee was spilled.
Only when goodnights were said did a little chill
escape the first, scrape a shoulder and stir her hair so

that she brushed it back with her hand
in a practiced gesture we would recall.
Living is like that, full of habit. We hoard
time for what needs thought. For example,
"Where did I put the pickles?" "Does this dress
make me look ridiculous?" Try to imagine it. Five
mortalities living as though there is no tomorrow
and a month later every one of them still alive.

The Joy of Cooking

She has prepared her sister's tongue,
scrubbed and skinned it,
trimmed the roots, small bones and gristle.
Carved through the hump it slices thin and neat.
Best with horseradish
and economical—it probably will grow back.
Next time perhaps a creole sauce
or mold of aspic?

She will have her brother's heart,
which is firm and rather dry,
slow-cooked. It resembles muscle
more than organ meat
and needs an apple-onion stuffing
to make it interesting at all.
Although beef heart serves six
her brother's heart barely feeds two.
She could also have it braised
and served in sour sauce.

You Are What You Eat

When she was a child
Mother was mashed
brains and poultry tails,
the throwaway parts
no one else wanted.
She grew up to be a secret
chocolate bar in a kitchen
drawer. When he married
Father was lamb
with blood at the bone
but toward the end
he was coddled egg.
When we met, my husband
was Peking Duck.
I was Greek olives, dark
and glistening near
the aperitif. Now he is
water and scotch
and I am one potato chip.

Appetite

No one in this family has ever died of
hatchet in a head or bullet in a back. Our love

and hate is such we look into each other's
eyes and chew. Withering looks and stifled furies

end with pass the mashed potatoes. It's not
the meat we love so much as appetite. The scents

attached. No one in this family models clothes
or suffers anorexia, our stomachs big

as beach balls. There are no whispered
stories of the cook's adultery, only criminal

assaults on the steaming lobster and sailors
gone to sea instead of jail for the thought

of mussels stewed in wine. Only the sacred
recipe for plum preserves from the dead Aunt

Ethel, pommes frites and steak, a bowl of blushing
nectarines, slathers of butter on raisin toast.

Religion

If you could see me picnicking one last time
at the crumbling table beside the park tower
you would know how I need the flavor of olives
and rough grained bread against the acid
of wine and Jack enjoying his peanut butter,
tasting the last of the chocolate-
covered ginger while the snow geese
dip their heads into the shallow water
and the fiery sun sets at five o'clock. You would
understand why I've no religion
but the ruddy duck and great white heron.
You'd see us divide the anjou pear in its perfect
ripeness and feel the chill air settle
into the hollow, watch as we zip
our sweaters with thousands of shore birds
in a quivering shifting cloud overhead
going nowhere in particular.
After an hour or two we would pack up
the picnic with only the pear core
and a small plastic box left over.
If you could see me picnicking
one last time where the plumed reeds
sway beside the park tower
you would know everything I know.

One Day Soon

The way each morning
you rise first and set
my orange juice out.

The way I find the crumbs
you dropped. I dust
the bentwood rocker, scrub
your tracked-in dirt.

The way you do the laundry
careful not to shrink
my shirts and run the stairs
to hang them up.

How at the grocery I avoid
tough crusts, remembering
your teeth.

The way you dig the garden,
bending down for me.
The way you clip the ivy.
Carry in the garbage cans.

The way I cut your hair
around the ears where
it grows thick and shave
your neck being careful
of the mole.

The way we read the paper
to each other. Talk
about the new gay
priest. The possibility
of key lime pie.

A Hard Piece on a Good Piano

What was maddening once is easy now by virtue
of practice, a hard piece on a good piano.

We are a community of two, sprung from the womb
in consecutive order. Mornings, I am up

before her. Finally, I hear her moan. These moments
have taken us seventy years. We sit for hours

not talking. There is a chance that if we speak
we won't get in. The lake bakes in the sun

but is cold deep down. Where the sheepmoss
sways. Where the lost keys lie. Between the house

and the lake, a broad lawn and stumps
the yardman marked with the sign of the fish.

I break off the worm, butter the corn
with fatted bread. She eats the tomato whole.

A heron stops on the beach to fish. We are
nearly alone. We have forgiven each other.

September in Bar Harbor

Then the hijacked plane flew into the tower. Again
and again, it flew into the tower. We didn't believe at first
but we saw. We saw. The ocean and trees were shimmering.
The cruise ship bobbed like a buoy on the sea. We sat together
for hours. A storm of ash. Sun flared from the sullied air.
When the hijacked plane flew into the tower
the New York pigeons flew up like a shot then settled again
some distance away. And a soft white dust coated

their wings. Is it all right to laugh and exercise? We get
our hair cut, ride a bike, call the children, dust
the sills. Buy some fragrant lilies for the table. Nowhere
are we free and yet we're free as birds. We are both
well and stricken with grief. Autumn has arrived but
the leaves won't fall the same. The earth is uneasy.
Is it appropriate to find home grown tomatoes and a dark
red onion for a casserole? Raspberries, the last of summer.

September 11, 2007

Love and Other Burdens

At last you understand your father, why
he turned up Galli-Curci on the phonograph

whenever you sang a love song
in your childish alto. He was not trying

to show you how; he was trying to drown you
out. It was he who gave you that first dose

of the unrequited—a father
who only took time for the best, a life-

long love affair with your mother. Help yourself
to another spoonful of sausage casserole

and forget who else might have fathered you.
Evidence is you are his child. You deny

yourself nothing, do not throw even
a compliment on the offering plate.

And no one expects more from you, a temporary
expression of DNA, imperfect vessel

at best who suffers broken symmetries.
Perfection exists in numbers. Not in heredities.

Falling Apart

It is him making a child's chair
with no grandchild crouched in a womb.
Carving the fragile flower
for an imagined back. Bending
the board to fit. It is him
walking two miles for a doorbell chime
in hopes someone will visit,
him at dawn leaning across the bed
to touch his wife awake. It is this wife
shopping for bread and milk
who buys a lemon pie instead. It is her
feeling blue on a golden day, gulping
pills the size of peony buds and choosing

white iris for the yard. It is her
who knows it should always be she,
her deliberate mistakes.
It is them sleeping side to side
in a double bed and dreaming safari,
embellishing at breakfast time
for mutual delight. It is them driving
cross-country at 5 a.m. These are theirs,
the torn chair, the scarred porcelain sink,
the bluebird he made forty years ago
for her birthday. Still at the table
picking corn from their teeth. The day
after giving the silver away.

In Which We Limit Ourselves

The pine wood is killed by the beetle.
We limit ourselves, say little,
walk by the prowling geese.
The wood duck is solemn.
Swans, mute. They fly synchronized
at first but then on an individual beat
like us—mated forever but still one and one.
For what was once orgy, we limit ourselves.
Two wild ponies graze by the lighthouse.
We don't get too close. Condominiums
sprout in the oat marsh. You point out
a colt by the road. I notice fawns
asleep in the grass. So many egrets
on Spartly Street with pale pink breasts
like big bleached robins. An ibis.
A tern. Across from McDonalds a yellow-
crowned heron, immobile. We watch
the bird for a while. Return
to the scarred brown ground, made ready
for seedlings. The land. The sky.
The birds. The sea. We bring home
only one shell. Limit ourselves to love.

A Life

A life that never wandered far from path
or road. One which consumed
a great many hot dead chickens
off shiny plates. Flowered. Blue-rimmed.
Then perfectly white. In this, a life with taste.
A life that believed in hope when its sharp toenails
made holes in its stockings. When it was bitten
by spiders. For wasn't it praised
for doing little or nothing? A life
that dusted the same table for generations
and failed to shake out the cloth. Wept
enough to make a lake and never befriended
a lifeguard. A life of laughter
at its own expense, thumbing through
the picture books of self, the slick magazines
of everyone else. A life that goes to bed with doubt,
whose sills are crammed with pencil jars
and ragged envelopes. A wobbly life, balanced
on one foot, hopping square to square. The other foot
just dangling there. Wretched, ecstatic.

Tundra Swans

Fog wrapped the shore where they must have drifted,
a thousand or more, stretching their necks into the haze.

Each probably had a kink in the neck where the body
met it. Each black beak probably sported a yellow spot.

We could only judge from what we'd read.
We could only hear them startle and bark.

Then the sound intensified. They rose into sight, wheeling
and honking, necks flat out, created an audible swish

as if each wore a taffeta skirt. We could see the bright fog
through their wings. When they got too high

they disappeared. They were hundreds and we, just two. Yet
they were individuals. Mated, for life. They would know

each other anywhere. In the fog or rain or night. I can
pick you out three blocks away. Your walk, the way you hold your head.

They could have met in Alaska in a fog like this, not decades ago
in an English class. She enjoys an occasional dragonfly. He eats

only greens, speaks to her in a radio voice. Sinewy, white,
between water and sky, they know where to go. Like us.

Curiosity

On the other side of the glass door not six feet
away from our dining room, the sharp-shinned hawk
was tweezing the black feather cap
from a chickadee he'd just caught. Then, breast
and tail feathers flew. He sat
on the new stump table we'd made
and after the plucking, pulled
the head from the carcass, gulped
the small bones. Pecked and chewed and swallowed.
I watched till chickadee fluff drifted the ivy
and nothing else was left. The hawk flew
up to the plum tree, his rusty, barred
plumage frilled by the wind. He was in view when
I sat down and took a bite of my tunafish sandwich
on rosemary bread. I chewed a chip. He looked
away. With one yellow foot, he scratched his neck.

Ecstasy

The immaculate sparrow comes every day
to bathe at eight o'clock. Looks around to judge
the risk, steps briskly into the bath and splashes
about. Steps out, savors it. Then in again.
Does a jig. Lifts a leg, a wing. Looks as if to fly
away. Changes its mind. In. Out. Can't get

enough. The sparrow's lookalike a branch
above but with no dark spot at the throat
displays no interest. Why not? Here is ecstasy
for the taking. And such a demonstration.
When finally the bather leaves, the waiting
bird flies down. Considers. Takes a little drink.

Aspects

New moon in the old moon's arms.
   Mirror spattered with paste and silver.
     My parents in their separate graves.
        The fire I tend to keep the predator away.

Quarter moon sawing the dark.
   Mirror cleaved in its silver.
     The children in their separate lives.
        Set fires. Fanned blazes.

Full moon shielding its dark twin.
   What I see is closer than it seems. More clever.
     The spent days. Injury and salve.
        Smoke taken for morning haze.

Gibbous moon, cloud-dimmed, foreign.
   The mirror in which I see forever.
     Valued friends: the cost, the haves.
        The ashes, like praise.

The White Bird

Nature exists without promise.
—John Berger

Beauty is not essential. Except
that the moon sheds bloomy light
over the freeway and tenements. Isn't snow
a useless dream of water? What does a butterfly
offer? A white bird carved to hang suspended
from a thread is only solace for the eye. Shelter
is a needed escape from nature. Prayer
is only for protection. Pain
is the first sign of life. But beauty
is for good measure.

Particulars

A rat in my garden, feasting
on daffodil bulbs. He stood
on his strong hind legs, peppy
as a prairie dog—looked as though
he owned the yard. I could not

deny it. The following day,
an overhead rustling in the house.
Birds, I hoped, in the chimney.
Looking out, the rat under
the plum tree. I bought a hat.

Put poison out. All day I couldn't
eat. I set a trap and thought
it snapped before it snapped.
One rat gives birth to a hundred
baby rats the size of honeybees.

I leaned on the sill. I could see
straight through the house
the way at times you look clean
through your life as if it is not yours
and holds no interest. A red car. A scrap
of leaf. The blur of a bird in flight.
Particulars, and yes, the world.

Looking Up from the Garden

Even in sun
after last night's
storm, even
with three kinds of roses—
in full bloom—
house and bodies are
quietly falling
apart. Grout squeezed
from between
the bricks. Flesh dropping
from arm bones
like flashing
slumped from the wall.

Words slow to come.
Doors that will not close.
Pillars of dust. Faucets
forever on
like fountains
at a gravesite.
One day the curious

will invade these ruins
where we'll lie mummified,
carvings of birds like dogs
at our feet—
their shrimp-fork toes
aloft. There will be

a memento shop
to sell replicas
of my cooking pots,
your recipe for wild tea.
Guides will raise
their umbrellas.

Here. Over here.
This is where
people were happy.

The Possum

This is the house where you cannot sleep.
This is the garden around the house
where the possum waits in the plum.
His sweet little face, eyelashes and nose
are wide awake. This is the house
where the mockingbird calls and the moon
refuses to say goodnight. This is the book
from the shelf in the house, the book the possum
will never read although you sit and stare
at its pages. This is a quiet peaceful house
within a block of town. The place you both
inhabit. Here, the sleepless possumy house.

The Body's Needs

All the refuse of a life sloughed off: the snot,
the spit, the cough, the shit, the laugh, the kiss,

the sweat. And all the demonstrated hurt:
the bruise and scratch, the rash.

Hard breath walking up a step, the vertigo of rise and fall,
the belly's acid fits. Hair, tears and nails.

But keep the touch, the push, the pulse, the copulation.
After-bliss. To look: the woodpecker, the worm. The ear

for thunder, singing voice and gasp. To see the elephant
and hear the owl. To walk from here to home and back

in a quickening of rain. The shade.
The fruit. The body's need for fat and thought.

And muscle-tone. The body's need for store-bought
teeth and hearing aides. The body's need

for getting rid. To rot. To smell. A pile
of bones and teeth and hair. Its homeless need to be

somewhere and then, its need to be nowhere.

The Reluctant Optimist

I put on the steamy July day, the perfect red rose
blooming on the infected bush. I forget
the idea of vodka and drugstore pills
and plan a letter of protest. Stop that project to stare
at an iridescent dish. Maybe today
after seventy years I'll be able to say I love my sister
without thinking "but." Maybe today
the seeds I planted will actually sprout
with rare black leaves or the irate neighbor will
bring me chocolate chips. If I looked in a hole
and saw a miracle instead of
a worm, maybe this life would wow me still.
I'll call my sister. Busy signal. So what.
I'll do the laundry. Look at the French
blue dress like evening sky. Look at the button-
holes frayed by a stretch of too-bountiful breast,
the golden stains from a breakfast of farm-fresh eggs.

The Long and Varied Lives of Breasts

One day she took notice of breasts, took time
for their strangeness. The way they swung down

when her mother dressed. How with her hands
Mother tucked them into the pockets of a brassiere.

She watched them swell on her sister, Fitz.
At night she would touch them when Fitz

slept. Her own flesh rising against her will—
she confronted the evidence, the fear

and derision from jokes, the need for notice
and also for praise. If her breasts were wanton

so were they shy. She was aware of their pleasure
at play. Their usefulness, apart from this.

Hilltop fountains that time in Trieste.
A landing. A nest. Still in their edgy

recklessness—a cry of "knife." So docile they lay,
like laughing girls in petticoats. So passive.

Freshly laid eggs. They drifted and phosphered
in her bath but turned to yeasty loaves in bed.

And when she was old, their skin more protected
and fair than cheek or belly or thigh,

she noticed the nipples alert, even to death.

Inheritance

for Debra

When the north wind reads the cherry's braille,
spins a few last leaves, and scours itself out
against the snow, that shelf where I keep our winters
tucked up in quilts, where the only warmth
is family, tells me "get in the car" and my tongue is stuck
again to the cold language of going home. Who says
there's been no progress? Here I am
with my micro hearing aid. My anti-acid pills.
Prozac. Acupunctured hip. Set the dead maple on fire
again, the part you drew three times
in leafy conflagration, the tree that showed us beauty
and desire while its roots lay dying underground.
I hear it's split to logs. Even such a tree in the summing
up is wood the way a body is water. What warms us
is material. The worn stuff left to survivors—
a dusty mulch of irony, a golden ring.

The Lover

So this is her lover, the one
who gets between her legs. Those legs
that kicked inside of me. Those legs

I dreamed when they were not.

So those are his eyes that take her in,
his breath that smells of apricots,
the very same he sighs

onto her breast. So he is the shore

she washed up on
after the long swim, the push
on the swing into spring air.

His is the face she might look for.

Mine is the face she nearly wears,
the smile she almost smiles. I am
the mother who conceived the daughter

who could love him. Her father sleeps

beside me. He is my one and only. Not
in the spring or any other season
have I ever looked across a room

and caught some other eyes upon me,

never run to meet someone in a dark
hotel or thrilled to stir my coffee with a spoon
he'd touched. The lover in this poem

is for my daughter, in case.

Motel

No private bath. A common
shower by the office. Pine boards
knocked together and a rusty
shower head inside
that wobbled on its stem.
A soggy bandaid in one corner.
Hair pin. Wadded condom. I reached

for soap and met with mine
his gleaming eye, dark
and pressed against a neck-high
knothole. His famished eye, taking in
my breasts and sex nest—shivery,
wet. The squalid gallery. His eye

on its own, the rest of him
relying. Beneath my nails a skim
of soap. Beneath my feet
the earth, the universe. In his eye
the speck of me.

Tequila Sunrise

I rented the movie but watching its love scene
with my grandson made me uneasy.
Tiny cold birds hopped about in my chest.
So much is hidden in the young. So much
they never say. For example,
what did Don Juan tell his mother?
She was grateful to know the name he called
his horse. I know the fish my grandson
will not eat. He knows I will not offer it.
Once he opened a door and saw me
naked in the shower. (Here they are,
dear heart, the weary breasts your mother
nursed from.) It was impossible. You had to
be there. Facing the music is counter-
productive in the case of the body. We watched
the movie stars, or were they stand-ins,
couple in the steamy tub, but later spoke
only of special effects. The drifts of vapor.
The pizza we ordered around midnight.

Local Anesthetic

A specialist, he operates
only on breasts. He squints
like a jeweler, cuts into her
flesh along the wire inserted
before. No, he is a general
and the slim wire is a pin
stuck in a war map. He asks
for a shears and he is a sculptor
finding the form. A sculptor
molding what's left of the breast
with sentient hands
as if she were a much younger
woman. He and the nurse talk
about movies. Consider

him three months later critiquing
the aureole, judging the scar,
admiring its color. Together
they praise the miraculous healing.
(There is a story he bent
once to kiss an incision.)

After she's dressed they talk
in his office. On the wall,
his honors diploma. By the phone
a desk pad printed
on every page with a lovely line
drawing of a breast.
Every convenience!

There is a Rumor

in the neighborhood
that I am dead—
dogwood berries
in a black squirrel's
mouth. Died
in her sleep
in the sun
they say, upright
in the garden
on a bench.

Well move, at least.
Write a letter.
Swear. Snap beans.

I cannot. I am
pinned
to the bench
like a donkey's tail
tacked by a dizzy
blind-folded
boy. Quite
off the mark.

This is the fiftieth
birthday
of my youngest child.

Circles

She was born this way. Twinned
smudges marking an otherwise common

face. A baby with circles under her eyes.
The whole of childhood she never looked

innocent. Darkness underscored
everything she saw. Her children born

were likewise marked—all
her descendents wear shadows

over their smiles.

Sophie's Face

Head propped in the bend
of my arm, dark eyes
squinched closed, the perfect
lips frame a yawn. Here a frown
unhooked to concern, a smile
without pleasure, a laugh
without mirth. All the expressions
mastered at birth but no experience.

How can we know
what a newborn dreams?
When will she learn
what grandmother is? I wait

for her to put her face to it,
language muscled in lips
and brow, the honest face
she will own for years
before, like me, she will learn
to hide what she feels.

The Straw House

At the end of my mother's life in the nursing home
she asked me to pull a wild hair from her chin mole.
It was the last thing I did for her. Just now, twenty years
later, feeling my chin—a stiff hair in my fingers. I go
to the mirror but my eyes are no good. I can't see
anything there. I take a knife from the pencil jar

and with the other hand, pull on the hair. At first I cut
the skin, so I let up a little. Then, I cut off an inch
but can still feel the stump. As if I were a wolf
howling in the woods among the pack, amid
restless shuffling and stinking pelts, I sniff
the persistent rot. As if I could blow down this house.

In My Element

Shell like a wrist bone, banyan tree seed pod split
almost in two, black acorn, lost to the pig. These artifacts

I've stolen away from an exotic place and saved
on a shelf to wonder at. Out of their element, I'd say.

Do they remember the silt of Africa, sunrise on a primitive
beach? And I? Should there be sea washing my bones

or mountains reaching my sky? Should there be oaks
or deserts and palms, stars and pyramids? Who was it

brought me here, so far away? In my element
I would be barefoot and loosely clothed. There would be

freshly cut grass for the smell and iris for looks, a river
and willows in spring. I would be taking my time. Reading

a poem aloud. Or riding a bicycle down the road. Later
there would be friends and family laughing at politics

in a half-lit room and a daughter with me in the kitchen
wrestling the carcass of the bird, liberating the wishbone.

Crone in Bloom

Pruned to a cripple, brittle
and black, Crone reaches out

like an addict for another spring.
In her ragged bark, memory

brings back the stab of flowering.
Where has her quick youth gone?

Would you still want to pause
beneath her branches,

the shade of her blossoms
so different from the shade

of leaves? Would it perch this year
at the top, her crow, its blot

of shining? Buds swell in the bends
of her trunk. Blossoms that can't be told

from blossoms of the young. Despite
the ache of aging, Crone

is once again in bloom
with blue-eyed grass about her feet

and on her tongue
a thin lozenge of moon.

Psalm of the Outcast Jew

Without consonant, the word for God is breath.
Trace it with your finger on the chalky slate.

Where the dust is gone it can hardly be read.
So it is that years ago for love of a man I married

outside the faith. Of twenty thousand days
with him I am glad. My roots cling to the riverbank,

exposed and gnarled. I dig at the clay. My leaves,
send word. Birds come and go with great variety.

Fifty years without mention in the house of my birth.
But the garden I live in is clipped and green, contained

in a circle of ironwood trees. I am the woman
whose death was told in a grandfather's prayer

when I was twenty. Day and night, seventy
years, the river of breath flows through me.

Dictionary of Occupations

Six nights a week Rose works as a chainpegger at her
doobyloom. Sam slaves all day as a butt presser. As a flitch-

hanger, Abe is unsurpassed. Then there's Joe, the retort forker
and Ida, the Panama hat smearer. Have you met the tangled

yarn spool straightener and the mother repairer? Does the sea-
foam kiss maker dance by the sea and who buys the soap

for the lingo cleaner? I am a word screwer, a thought aborter.
A red-throated irony pecker. You are a seven-miles-

to-coffee walker, a grammarpuss, a dust-dragger and bagger.
You are an amorous breast-patter and neck-kisser.

I am a nocturnal elbow stabber. I make you peanut
butter. You, you are such a quiet manner.

Late for Death

Death is busier every day. In Africa
and at the war. Earthquakes. Floods

and hurricanes besides his regular
day to day. I eat a chocolate, peel

an orange. Death checks his watch. I hear,
he says, you were also late for birth.

And the mid-life crisis you didn't have
until sixty-four. Late to hate and late

to mourn. We are having dinner guests.
Talking loud. Playing jazz. Death

is such a malcontent. I fondle his balls.
Surprise, he says, over the noise.

Wait, I say. I'm learning French. I'm not
in shape. Death eats dessert and a Tagamet.

My Haircutter Goes on Vacation

He is sun-bathing in Argentina and I
am going around with my head
bowed. He is walking his little blind
dog on the beach and I am forced
to wear a hat. Another woman in the shop
volunteers to cut it. How does she know
what I want? I can't explain it. Will she be
sympathetic to my tragic face, the flat
back of my head where my parents
let me sleep too much when I was a baby?
Or will she lay bare my balding
temples? My hair is curly where I want it
straight. My hair sticks out
where I want it flat and it is flat
where it should stick out. My hair
is a dull dull brown with gray creeping in
where the dye is gone. I put
the life of my hair in her hands. She is clacking
her scissors, sharpening
her razor. She can't wait to get
at it. She is snapping a towel to hang
on my neck. I tip my head
backwards over the sink.
She could slit my throat
while she rubs my temples. Don't
worry, she says. It will grow back.

Rain from a Cloudless Sky

Forgive me, vigor, for feeling logy in the morning. Heat,
forgive me air conditioning. My apologies
to hungry children for my low calorie diet. Forgive
my independence, women in Afghanistan. Forgive
me, heartbeat, for ignoring you. And breath,
for not enjoying you. Excuse me, Van Gogh,
for trying to paint my daughter's portrait. Pardon me,
husband, for eyeing other men with interest; pardon me,
other men, for preferring my husband. My apologies
to actors for thinking I might do better in the death scenes
and to Stephen Sondheim for preferring something
I can hum. Bear me no ill will, Wisława Szymborska,
for stealing your idea for this poem. Your originality.
Your intelligence. My kleptomania and neediness.

Charm School

"What are you thinking?" the art instructor said.
"I'm trying not to think," I answered
painting my face on the canvas black,
painting the doorway red, half afraid
of drowning in violet. "Your husband looks
so pink," said the painter on my right,
the one who listens to talk shows.
"He looks like a woman," said the painter
on my left, the one who brings her dog.
"Does he really have that much
curly hair?" said the instructor. "No,
he is mostly bald." I painted my husband's
face aquamarine. Painted my gray dress
green with maroon around the neck.
There on the palette a puddle of white,
a pool of black. Night tree in moonlight.
Death looked over my shoulder. Make
everything yellow, he said.

Snow and Circumstance

for Moshe Dor

From the moment he clapped
eyes on her black bangs
and canted brows. From the moment
she made a smart remark
and took her hand back
for a little slap. From that first
meeting of lips there was no
moderation. There was no wife
or money or fame or friends. Almost
no country. People who knew him

tasted the news like a custard.
Sweet and viscous, it stuck
to their tongues. Such a love.
We all deserve it.

What is it he cares about?
Not lies that are told
to be polite. Not the fact
that nobody knows he is famous.
Not twenty inches of snow
and Jupiter has no water.

She comes home from work
and nibbles his fingers. Or
they hold hands in the car.
He cannot get used to this
weather. But there she is
in a black brassiere, so cute
at fifty. She will be cute for him

at sixty-five sprawled
on a blue velvet couch.
Reupholstered. Her ears, fresh
bread. Her lips a fine blackberry
jam. For the rest of the world,
another snow fall. For the rest
of the world, other loves.

What Mattered Then

The family, mid-picnic—sister looking coy (she will marry
a judge), brother bemused (he will be famous almost
at once), mother and father uncomfortable sitting
on the ground (they are in it now). Collision in the air
like exhaled breath, intimate as resemblance. Our lives
full of dust and us shaking them out. Long moments composed
of confusion. A sunny day. The naked cherry tree, but full
of potential springs. The accelerated car on the way to God knows
where. The soundless trembling of needles on the pine. What was
in the air? I have forgotten. The grit of what mattered then.

Long Marriage

An excellent marriage in retrospect
if not always at the moment.
A few pulled teeth.
Infirmity but not of the mind.
The saved $5 when it counted;
the hundreds spent for a mask
in Venice. In addition, friends
in Des Moines. Belonging without
ever being possessed. Oh, she wears
a gravy-stained dress
in companionable silence, confident
that he will spot a ripped seam
when she changes to go out.
They both enjoy chopped meat
but not for fifty years do they agree
on garlic. This is monotony
transformed by nuance. No subtlety
is ever too much. He always
sees a bright side. She
never forgets what the matter is.

Jack Was Going Out the Door

Oh, I love you and love you not.
Marry you and unmarry, hold you
and put you out. Oh, I taunt you
and I want you, too. And the season
of autumn that comes too soon
too late too many too few, goes
wintering away. Goes springing,
blue. And the night is light and warm
and old. Its buttons are bright
and brass. Its sleeves too long, its
body too tight. Oh, I hold you to bed
and throw you out. I love you
and not with all of my might.

The Bird Book

A gull knows the same
man after he's been away,
after he's married again
and become allergic
to bees. Some green herons

drop bread in the water

to bring up fish. Sanderling
legs are a blur to the eye.
Their feet leave no prints. The ibis
are standing on their toes.
That is their ankle, not

their knee. Storks can catch fish

with their eyes closed because they hunt
by touch. Except for ptarmigan,
grouse are polygamous. New feathers
appear they do not choose. Birds
are forever pink or black

or blue, violet, white, yellow

or green. Brown or red
or speckled or striped.
Do they flock together
depending on color? Depending
on size and habit? On song?

The way we began.

The way before thought
we slept and ate, made love
and sounds and grabbed
with our hands and walked
and ran and wore our skin.

The Sweet Comfort of Denial

Maybe I shouldn't tell this about my mother
but she got out of her wheelchair

when no one was looking. Dancing
always made her happy. She kept a secret

chocolate bar in the kitchen drawer. Maybe
I shouldn't tell this about my father but he held

his hands limp at the wrist. He could have been
gay! It didn't matter. He laughed

and laughed at his own jokes. And once
I cheated, counting votes to make myself

a prom queen. I was a knockout in a dress
from Marshall Field's. Marriage to me has meant a lot

to my husband. He broke his rib and got a hernia
by falling down the stairs in Florida

carrying my beach chair, but he got right up
to take my picture with a pelican.

Even with luck gone sour. Even with a dead brown wren
on the steps and the lights out. It is dark as the inside

of a gravedigger's sleeve. A snow storm dumps 24
inches after an Orange alert. Still, we listen to Chopin

on the battery radio, eat blue cheese
and crackers, touch hands on the couch. Marriage

to my husband has meant a lot to me. The end
of the world is approaching but we are elated

because a neighbor has shoveled our walk.

The Ingenuity of the Damned

Signs of life on a meteor from Mars. Water
on Jupiter's moon. Dredged
logs from the lake, surfaced from worlds
of current and cold, yesterdays
counted in circles and scars. Greatness
and despair in the arrangements of words.
The leaf that splits the rock.
Blossoms from a desert cactus.

The Good Lord Sees a Shrink

So you worked hard for seven days
How do you feel about that?

You have it wrong. On the seventh day
I rested. Had a piece of honey cake.

But how do you feel
about what you've made?

Things began to go wrong. The snake.

What comes to you when you say
Snake?

I worked so hard
on his fancy coat. Perhaps the way
he talked to man. And the apple
was so know-it-all.

Let's talk about apples now.

It was the whole of life itself,
the choosing, the color, flesh
against the teeth, juice running
down. The stiffened core and then
the seeds from which will come
again, the tree.

Do you like apples yourself?

I enjoy them. When catastrophe
strikes I like to eat.

What makes you so sad?
(There's Kleenex on the desk.)

I made mistakes. For example: man.
What comes to man when he says God?

Haircut

I get it short. He sprays it. I walk out

onto the avenue. Do I want to look
like this—well groomed as a poodle,
tarted up, employed. An expert

on closet organization? I come home
and rearrange it. Push some hair
around, inspect my balding temples.

No matter what I do or how, they show.
I fool around till I look like me—messy
as a wind-blown tern, full of fish, nothing

to do but sit or fly for the hell of it.

Superwoman

Awakening to orange juice and toast.
Reading the Style section. Eating

leftover bean soup. Taking a walk.
Writing an email to Debra, my daughter.

Reading a library book. Opening
windows. Laughing out loud. Taking my pills

with three glasses of water. Visiting
the shrink. Eating potato chips.

Singing, "Buddy Can You Spare a Dime?" Taking
another nap. Snacking on chicken wings.

Doing all this flying around. Sooner or later
I'm going to have to fight some evil.

My Mother, If She Had Won Free Dance Lessons

My mother was suspicious if she won anything at all.
Nothing is free, she said. One way or another, you have to pay.
A gift meal in a restaurant. But the steak is tough.
A gratis dress but it was made of cheesy stuff.
She had arthritis and couldn't stand without help.
But what if just once she spun around the room,
forgetting her knees, her helpless hips. Maybe my father,
the business man, would cradle her torso, swaying
across the dance floor as if *Dancing with the Stars*. Throwing
her out and around, bending her back over his arm
till the heavens swooned. Maybe my father
turned out to be expert at tango. He stared
into her eyes. She would put on three-inch heels
in Argentina. There she would stamp her foot.
How the gauchos would applaud and doff their black hats,
put them over their hearts.

My Mother Couldn't Breathe

The man next door showed off.
He could jump a broomstick, lift

me high and throw a football

so it floated down the street. His wife,
Cerise, could run and run around

the block. We played till dark, had breath

enough to blow a saxophone, smoke
a Lucky Strike, to bottle lightening

bugs. To weep. Mother stayed

inside. To ward off demons, devils,
witches, she wore a copper coil

around her neck. It left a greenish

ring. She lit a dish of sulphur
in the hall and sniffed. I needed

her to braid my hair. She held me

close and wheezed into my ear.
I pressed my face into her breast.

She had a scratchy kiss. A gasp.

A choke. A stiff hair in her mole.
My mother couldn't breathe.

Lost

We were young the last time
we came to see the migration.
Then the sky disappeared as the birds
rose up, their quarrels shrill, a rustling
taffeta sound, feathers pale
against the sky. We could see their black
faces and yellow spots. The noise
outdid the wind and they covered both sides
of the bridge.

This time the gusts
blew hard. An eagle passed. A ladder
leaned against a tree but there was
no observer. The air was cool.
Leaves hung bronze, all but the maples
which clung to red. Where were the birds?
Had they taken a new route out of boredom?

We were lost. The small motel.
The water across the street.
What used to be as if it never was.

Good Things

There is a full moon.
I got my driver's license.
We had French toast for breakfast.
Went up on the roof for sunshine.
Slept soundly all night.
Drank my three glasses of water.
Jesse and Elizabeth are in love.
Barbequed brisket in the food section.
Maker Faire in California.
Got in to feed the cats.
Open house at Deb's school.
Ross helped her with a ladder.
Going to get a cortisone shot.
I'll be 82 on the second.
Sarah's for breakfast.
With my new license I can drive
until I'm 90. But I'm getting tired
of Scrabble.

Falling in Love

In the years past sex, past children, past hearing and thinking,
we became so close we coalesced, words migrating

like blood. Your trips to the grocery for pie crust and margarine
were like long voyages to Greece. You were seeing islands,

watching the fishermen and birds, eating at a table by the wharf.
I asked about everything you saw. A dog barking was news.

You brought me a bottle of wine. A happy four-year-old
escaped from the preschool. We were traveling without a ship.

The train, late again. And smells. An apartment full of bouquets.
The refrigerator and pantry stocked with rubber-banded packages

of what is left. Since we were young we have been together.
You called up to get addresses, squinting at the small numbers

in the phone book. I copied out the system. You studied
the stars. We wanted to know the balances. How much

had we spent? This winter was just days away and yet
we honored every tree. Played Scrabble in the park.

Took pictures of each other as if we had nothing
but time. Planned to send out holiday cards.

Knowing What Jack Gilbert Knew

We were visiting Zion outside
Virgin in Utah. Surrounded by Mormons.
Deer gathered and wolves
howled. I wrote poems and read
Jack Gilbert. Wanted to learn what he knew.
I recorded fifty days of hiking and eating
and reading and writing. How happy
we were. Today is not so different. But we are not
as happy, reading and eating and writing.
Do the deer still gather?
Do the wolves still howl? Do the Mormons
still believe? Woke up and then went back to bed.
Snow dusted the streets and trees.
I think I know what Jack Gilbert knew.

Poetry in Bulgaria

was more popular, the Bulgarian
poet said, when the public
had to read between the lines. Sly
metaphors—when a honey bee
gone berserk robbing the hive
or a hummingbird
mooing like a cow
was really the oppressor.
Then poetry was exciting.
Then art was private protest
and needed to be read.
Then copying machines
were controlled by government
and copies were impossible
to get. Now there is a much smaller
audience, almost indifferent.
Possibly, they are right.

What Deer Will Eat

Yarrow and monkshood, dame's
rocket, rock cress deer will not eat
for love or money. Spruce and juniper,
holly grape deer will not eat, even
in evening with a full moon. Barberry, astilbe,
bleeding heart deer will not eat on the warmest
day in spring when you dream meadows
and true love appears. But periwinkle

and English ivy, trillium and violets
deer will nibble and tear at
there by the salt lick, there by the pool.
Korean Lilac, hydrangeas for them
are roast chicken and wine. For dessert
you can serve them crabapple trees.

Astilbe, bleeding heart, bearded iris, deer
will not eat in a war zone, even in peace.
Dead nettle, lamb's ears and holly grape
deer will resist. The common lilac will bloom
undisturbed. The whole mustard family is left
to thrive except wallflower and candytuft.
Deer will shun buttercups on the path, but
the turban flower makes a nice snack.

The Young

There is much to be done.
The country is deep in debt.
The war must be stopped and gas
prices go up and down. It will take the young
to make the changes. But they are busy.

Every day they take a picture
of themselves and put it on
the internet. Tune in. You can discuss
what they are wearing.

They are the new constituents. It is time
for change, the politicians say, and hope.

This doesn't affect
the middle-aged who are still
obsessed with the Middle East. It doesn't affect
the old busy frying up
mushrooms and onions
for lunch.

It doesn't affect the dog who has stepped
on a bee and needs to go to the vet

or the bee who because of the dog has suffered death.
It doesn't affect the stars which startle us
on cloudless nights or the clouds which at times
obliterate their shining.

There is much to be done.
Get busy, if you're young.

The Limp

His teacher was a cripple too—a basketmaker
tramp from the village beyond. All you need

is a blade, he said. A place to work. Bamboo
is free and fast to grow. Often the height

of an eight-year-old in a day. Some baskets
he weaves to spill not light: baskets for tea

or packs to shoulder that fit the back.
But into this he weaves the day. A basket

for carp. A sieve to trap better than hands, more
than a belly would want. It holds a weight

as easily as the fisherman's eyes contain
the sky. He does not blame the new

factory that parodies his work. He does not
ridicule the plastic reds and blues.

Those baskets are cheap and quick
to make. Without the limp, he says, I might

have married, had a son. I might have
worked on a farm or made a good wage in Tokyo

hinging the doors on Toyotas. They call him
"National Treasure" now. His baskets,

art. If I were born today, he says,
they would know how to fix a limp.

The Unfinished Poem

I keep putting new lines at the end
of my unfinished poem, trying them on

like coats, for goods and looks, some
buttoned up, one or two zipped, a few open

showing the dress beneath. I keep
showing the poem and getting a lot of

advice. This poem is wearing too much.
This is a cold poem. This poem appears

to have nothing under its flowered coat.
I tack my unfinished poem to the wall.

Whenever I enter the room, there
it almost is. A letter from my dead mother

about loving too much, a caution light
on New York Street, a menu but no

wine list. Even in my dreams I hear it:
"Sing to me," it says, "I can't sleep."

In the Mirror

Consider the cagey face, trying
to see itself but hoping
to give nothing away to its merciless
observer. A futile enterprise
but also a tribute
to the human spirit which never expects
less than a miracle.

Babel Reunion

And it came to pass that peace
was withheld from them
because of their many tongues—
in every translation there was a quibble,
in every word a different shade.
And it was remembered how
once at Babel words were enough;
they built a tower of earth
and slime nearly to heaven. And so
it happened they planned a reunion.
Invitations embossed with the tower,
the unmistakable landscape of Shinar,
were sent to the builders' descendants
scattered over the world. A dance
was planned. A million exotic dishes
were tasted and sprinkled with parsley.
The tower ruin was topped
with a searchlight. Everyone came
including babies. Myriad voices spoke
at once in countless tribal slangs
so a cloud of noise rose up,
then settled slowly—a mantle of silence.
In the heat the descendants removed
their garments and stood in the dust,
skins stained every color of earth.
They looked around to see
who had inherited Eve's broad hips.
They looked around to see who was
circumcised. Someone remembered
the old Babel jokes. They laughed
and cried. And God was not afraid.

The Cry

Having sent his wives and servants on ahead,
and his eleven sons (where had the daughters gone?)
and all his herds, Jacob thought he was alone,
but moonlight showed his angel

sat beside him. They had a bit of cheese
and bread, then entertained themselves
with wrestling games. The angel's head rode
high in the crook of Jacob's arm and his nostrils

flared pale with exertion. The angel's feet
made no sound, nor were they visible
but hid inside a knee-high mist from which
white birds flew out. His hands were strong

on massive arms that matched his frame.
And Jacob's guile, the guile that mottled
sheep and goat to swell his herd, the guile
that charms to Rachel gave so he would know her

in the bed, bid him bite his angel
on the lip as if they were both human.
What a sound the angel cried—before
he lightly touched the top of Jacob's thigh

and it was out of joint. Across the river,
huddled near a tent, Leah
thought the angel's cry was Jacob's coming
from his bed. It was more ecstatic and more

lightning-sent than in her own experience.
She knew jealousy. I hate his lust, she said.
This made her sister, Rachel, smile.

Leah Complains to God

Weak-eyed Leah steps on the hem
of God's garment to hold him and tell
how Jacob neglected her during the sandstorm,
busied himself with camels, then called
to her sister, Rachel, in a loving tone.
And I am the eldest, Leah complains.
She says she discovered a niche
where fifteen staffs lay nested
and glistening, arranged by size.
He is compulsive, she says to God.
The tent must be spotless; he prefers
silence. His obsessions make my life hard.
Then leave him to Rachel, says God.
I cannot. I want him. Last night
he refused me, took the stone pillows
to build a pillar he doused with oil.
This was for You, God. Jacob
does nothing for me. Calm yourself,
Leah, says God. The story
is just unfolding. Leah protests:
how can You say that?
We are well into the plot.

Fragile

After death, the angel says, look back. You can see the footprints of your life. But there are places where the footprints disappear. The angel says, that's where I was carrying you.
—John Berger

On the walk I watch the cracks, the places
mended with tar, the little bumps
for the blind. Over the oven
I bend cautiously to get the pans.
And in the shower one hand on the towel rack. Getting
into a car I carefully put
my foot. And when I go where I go
to sleep, in the very first house, like a china cup
about to be dropped on tile. Like a dried leaf
in wind. Like a kiss blown by lips
after the loved one has turned away.
I lie with my head on my husband's arm
so his angels will catch me when I fall.

Greatness and Despair
in the Arrangement of Words

Forks full of white potatoes
talked about, sunlight
on a rosy flower
described. While pleasures
of great moment cruise
to Martinique—I call
from shore, happy
with my choice of how to say
goodbye. And what

you speak on waking
is as loving as a touch.
Better than signs of life
on a meteor from Mars.
Letters saved and books.
Apologies. A thought
engraved upon a watch.
Whether spontaneous
or wrought, each
from the simple alphabet
of greatness and despair
assembled and arranged.

From

On Hogback Mountain

(1985)

The Mother in Line 28

The poem is not the poet.
The mother in line 28
is not the poet's mother or child
and each time a poem opens a door
to a room of pans or pearls
it is the poem's room;
it is the poet's plan.

The heart that is bleeding
in stanza two
is not the heart of the poet.
The poet is elsewhere,
singing along with a piano player.
The heart in the poem won't heal.
The poet's own heart is strong.

The Truth About Bears

The old bear plays a game much like quoits;
he splashes water rings over the lake.

Slim trout rise to rub noses with air;
the tracks they leave are round as moons.

The old bear waits for the fish that is strong,
rash, obsessed with the meaning of bear.

When the strong fish springs like a trap from the lake
his tail strikes the bear with the strength of ten fish.

The force of the fish hits the bear
like the brush of a wing or the scratch of a twig.

The bear strikes the fish with the strength of one bear.
For a moment the bear holds the fish in his mouth

alive. Fish against fur is paler than berries
before they burn blue. In the eye of the fish

is the truth about bears.

Mrs. Venture Advances

Mrs. Venture advances, holding her bric-a-brac bones
out to the sidewalk ice, betting her legs
on the three-buckle boots she bought in the blizzard of '50.
At the corner she mails to Vermont an order
for daffodil bulbs, then shuffles an inch at a time
to the drug store to sit at the counter.
She is friends with the counter girl, Hattie.
Mrs. Venture lives without cats in the house Henry bought
before he died. When they were children
they ran off together in spite of his mother.

Her favorite grandson eloped
with an older woman, divorced from the mailman.
Dottie, her daughter, tried to protect her:
"Mama, he's gone joined the Navy.
He took his guitar picks and left."
Old Mrs. Venture turned toward the wall
where the cobwebs shook in the air from the heat vent.
She smelled a lie as quick as a fart in the closet.
"He'll be all right, Dottie," she said. "He's a good boy."

Mrs. Venture Does the Two-Step

The rose safety-pinned to her bodice
is the hardiest bloom she could find,
cut from the climbing vine back of the house,
the same vine that screens the trash can,
tangles the lilacs and blossoms in the fig.

As they dance, her partner, the carpenter man
who can fix anything made of wood, is aware
that the merest brush of his shirt on her dress
and the rose will be lost. He holds her clear out,
looks over her shoulder, admires the grain in the wood
on the bandstand. Untouched, the red petals
fall to the floor like bits of a thin, dark glove.
Old Mrs. Venture, strong as gin punch, presses
the rest of the rose to her partner's chest.

Mrs. Venture Deals with Crime

The window is open.
She is breathing the little green flames
that burn in her every spring.
She sips at herb tea from the thin cup
that used to hold whiskey before
she got healthy. Old. Mrs. Venture
gestures to Henry, though he's been dead
seven years, but as her arm lifts
she sees through the window a peeper
standing on daffodils, ogling
her blue blanket robe, her hair net.
Old Mrs. Venture picks up
a petit point doorstop made from a brick.
"If you want entertainment, go to the movies,"
she shouts to the peeper. "A man of your age."

Mrs. Venture Buys Time at a Health Club

The masseuse wears a white cotton suit.
On Mondays, Bavarian Bertha, the greeter,
has her mouth crimped for the rest of the week.
Claire, a dark beauty who picks up the towels,
converses in English, Spanish and French,
describes how to perk up the hair
with jelly of egg and oil pressed from almonds.
Old Mrs. Venture rubs the gray mess
into what's left of her hair.
It turns stiff as an egg box.

In spite of the warning on age, old Mrs. Venture
enters the steam room. Women like clouds
just after sunset, rise from a tier of wood benches—
bellies, arms, legs in cumulonimbus. The bone
of her hip hurts from the bench. Mrs. Venture
runs her palms down her sides where skin hangs loose.
She touches herself, remembering flesh. At this summons
the vapor of Henry appears and, rising, shakes
hot rain on her breast.

Outside the steam room there is a picnic hamper
of ice. Mrs. Venture holds ice to her neck
as she watches herself in the mirror. In the same
frame is a dancer creaming muscular legs.
Old Mrs. Venture sees herself dancing the tango.

Good Girl

I know what a good girl is.
I have been a good girl,
flattered those who scorn me,
listened hours to a bore.
I do anything to please.
I shut my mouth,
feel guilty on demand.
I know what a good girl is.

I am such a good girl,
I dress up in a plain brown wrapper,
at parties I don't mix with men,
I would never kiss my doctor.
I know what a good girl is.

I will be a good girl,
smile until my mouth aches.
I will not tell the truth.
I will not tell the truth.

Letter Home

Father,

I have been named toad and whore
by children and nuns and have not
fought back, have not until now
called them bitches,
those sweet-faced pets of yours
whose hearts are sharp as shovels.
When I am silent ice limbs climb
my chest, feed on my knees
and numb my feet.

When I speak, ingratiating lies unfold
like linen handkerchiefs, bleached
and creased as though my mother ironed them.

Now I am told I will never hear, till death,
a lemur sing, or sit in Charleston
sipping drinks with friends.

Madness, they say, has its own delights
and does not need the help of woman or man.
Father, who throws me over
the ravenous sea, catch me.
I have had such trouble.

Dear Elaine,

We receive thousands of letters every day, each heartfelt
and worthy of response. It is impossible, however,
to write letters to every one who seeks answers to problems.
Be assured that your letter has been read with interest.

Galesburg

(*Homage to Richard Hugo*)

I thought I was going to Clinton, but I came to Galesburg by mistake.

I never complained.

I complain loudly and to everyone.

The people are expecting me. They have come out of stores on Main Street carrying gifts. I am overwhelmed by the gifts. They are all ties. It is hard to seem properly grateful as I do not wear ties.

There is an Italian grocery on most blocks and the competition in pasta is cutthroat.

There is a lot of kissing on street corners and there are bridges over the rivers for lovers. People who are not lovers must cross the rivers by wading. High purple boots are the fashion.

I meet the mayor at a church supper even though I am Jewish. He shared his knishes with me. They were delicious.

In Galesburg you must get a job when you are fourteen unless you are blonde. Blondes get to live by their hair alone and spend their time combing and braiding.

I am happy even though I am not blonde.

I am miserable and try to dye my hair but it turns orange.

Women on the street must carry cakes. Some cakes are in the shape of old automobiles. Others are shaped like men.

Women who never married have a club in the town. They are the judges and give strict sentences to married women.

I enjoy just walking the streets of the town. There is an old bicycle tire factory that smells strangely of oleander or cooked celery.

There is a street on which everyone must shut his eyes. There is a guide rope for hands and a place where there is a community of hands meeting. It is a rule that no one must speak there.

I spoke there once and was criticized.

I spoke there once and enjoyed the startled hands my speech inspired.

I spoke there once and was run out of town.

I never spoke there but always wanted to.

There is an institution for the mentally ill where everyone goes two days a week. Each townsperson must either serve as a doctor or patient during these two days. People get to decide for themselves which it will be.

Autumn comes and goes but no one notices.

It is against the law in Galesburg to drive a foreign car.

Foreign visitors are each given a Ford for a gift. This practice is becoming a financial burden for the town.

I have made plans to leave. I have been planning to leave for fifteen years.

Twice I have bought tickets for points west.

I will never leave. There are no roads out of town.

There are so many roads out of town it is difficult to decide which to take. It is easier not to go.

Clinton, 1942

Mother made chicken soup.
Our bowls were ringed with gold.
They were as wide as Mother's face
and our spoons dripped scalding broth.

As we ate, farmers loafed
in front of the store.
It was open for business.

Hitler screamed on the radio.
Mother sold a green coat
to a woman whose son
was at the age to go.

That summer I minded the store
in a grasshopper storm.
Grasshoppers stuck to the windows
and drifted against the door.
And I shovelled them into a sack, like bones.

Zolana

Flat-chested town along the Mississippi past McKenna Field,
no ticket needed to the county courthouse.
Slap the marble floors, rub your back along the cold red stones,
use the bathroom free.
You might see Zolana powdering her chin moles.

Zolana ran the counter at the courthouse cafeteria.
She was my friend when I was in fifth grade
and thought that only Jews got breasts.
That was the year I read King's Row with hands cross-cupped
against my chest in Zolana's living room.

We stood together naked for the front hall mirror,
she a woman fully, I becoming,
two models longing for a painter.

She touched my breasts
and spoke in thin anticipation of brassieres,
the tyranny of motherhood, the proud mouths of lovers.

Zolana, it is better than you said.

Death

It is like I am in high school
and all I can think is when is Death coming
by the window of the Latin class.
He wears outrageous pajamas
and will mess up the bathroom.
Who would clean it up once I went out with him?
Who would fix the snack afterwards
when he is hungry from such vigorous dancing?

When he finally walks by the windows
he is with someone else,
my mother. He is squeezing her shoulders
and they have a joke between them.
It is wonderful to hear my mother
laugh again. I am not jealous.

Amo, amas, amat, amamus.
She is wearing his red and black sweater.
She has his class ring.
I am giving Death to her.
I am touching hands with Billy Sternberg
who edits the yearbook
and can tell a hundred jokes.

On Hogback Mountain

The crickets are loving their legs,
the blue jay is pestered by sparrows,
the mountain is sounding.
A snake, got up like an argyle sock,
crosses the trail.
I stick to my rock.
The snake loops out
like a Chinese buttonhole
just as a boulder lets go of the ridge
with a sound that picks up
all the other sounds by the skin of their necks.
The whole tribe of noise shoves off
down the mountain for Boise.

It is more quiet than you can imagine.
The crickets, the blue jay, the sparrows, the snake
all are still.
My eyes are pinned close by surprise.
It is the crickets who notice first
that they are all right.
Then the sparrows.
The jay isn't sure and the snake
buttons himself to a lichened knob.
I go to the edge of the ridge
and look over.

Wet

It rains inside,
water rises two flights.
Outdoors the elm
trolls back and forth
catching at glass
in the window.

We wring out our lives,
tie a corner of yours
to me and over the bedpost,
throw them over the sill
and jump.
We land in Mexico

drunk. I wear red silk
in the morning
and sequined sneakers.
The water is up to our waists
and rising. You say
I am beautiful wet
and we share a bottle of beer
and a taco plate.

Red snappers kiss at my sneakers.
You dive in your
three-piece business suit,
come up with a fish
in your teeth.
It slaps at your bridgework.
I troll my shoes in the stream.

Rodeo

Out of the gate of the womb
into the ring I ride
female.
I can do anything.
By the time I am five
I can lasso the cat,
lean over the hose to drink,
bring my wet chin to my sleeve
like a cowhand.
By seventeen I earn a good living
from the back of a horse
picking up handkerchiefs,
sweeping the dust with my teeth.

The slippers I wear in the paddock
are a gift from my daughter,
Carma Lu
who plays harmonica in and around Chicago.
At thirty-two she is my youngest.
When she was four she played Clair de Lune
on rubberbands.

Once a year I meet Sid
at a club in Chicago where Carma Lu plays.
It is a shock seeing his face again,
feeling his hand on my neck,
having him ask me again if I'm ready
to settle in to a house in East Quincy.
I tell him the prizes I won
in Cheyenne.
We have a few beers and Carma Lu plays
"Chicago Rock Clair de Lune."

Refusing the Eye

Eye roots run deeper than the roots of teeth.
Eyes branch on the palms of hands,
show beneath fingernails, walk on the tops of feet.
Each of the senses spends on the eye—
smell trades a breath of snow for the eye's ice crystal,
vectors of rose are gifts from a voice.

I became solely engaged in seeing.
I could see cells in human skin
as they moved. I could map exhalations of birds
in flight and discern the half-sweat
that precedes hesitation.
My friends avoided me.
Out of loneliness, I refused the eye,
relied on the interior sense of touch that is feeling.
Now withered roots of sight deprive me
of properly tasting and hearing.
No oranges rise up from the moons of my nails
and my hands holding music could be handling newsprint.
Except for the flower ends of the organ
which faint behind lids,
there is nothing with which I can see.

Last Child

After the fire
men lived on the desert,
women lived near the mountain
where there was shade.
All other land was flattened and melted.

Whatever was spared by the fire seemed holy.
The herb, rosemary, sprang from between the rocks on the mountain.
With its bruised leaves women perfumed the skin
of the last child on earth.

The child had seen miracles—
once a small bird.
She had seen stars
and color in water.

She was told by the women
that she would give birth to a child.
They taught her the way it is done.

When it was time, the man was a stranger.
He had come far for this
the old woman told her.
They straightened her hair,
held on to her shoulders.

The man touched her body in places,
gathered the scent of rosemary
as though he, too, were a child.
The old women moaned; their eyes were open.

On the gray desert a mist arose
like a field of white iris.
From the bald mountain a mist descended.
Between the last child and the woman she was becoming
there was a clearing, a place of flowers.

Words Have Sex Lives of Their Own

She undressed her words
so their bones would show
and joints would move
in unusual ways.
The words turned around,
they made love in her mouth.
What a coup for the language.
The chaste in the room
effervesced from their ears,
changed their minds
to erogenous zones.
Every sentence they spoke
knew a sensuous root,
every phrase
kept a sentence or two
on the side. Every word,
it was learned, had once squealed
with delight in the bed,
with delight in the bed of the mind.

From
Blameless Lives
(1992)

Reunion

A woman says goodbye to her husband
and hurries to her high school
reunion. Even after forty years
some things remain the same.
There is George. She nudges his hip
with hers, touches his hair, his knee,
his hand. He seems little changed
from the boy who jitterbugged with her
on the veranda of the Pythian Sisters'
Home. Because he is one of the few
who live hard lives without changing
expressions, she does not know he has
a retarded child, an alcoholic wife.
He does not know how rich she is and happy.
At ten that night they find the riverfront
park dark as a damson plum. With considerable
effort they climb the chain link fence
of the municipal pool, an overweight
fifty-eight-year-old woman and an arthritic
fifty-eight-year-old man. She discards
her lavender dress like a tissue.
He removes his seersucker suit and folds it
on the grass. In the darkness they look
at each other. Maybe the yearbook was right
and they are the cutest couple.

On the tower diving board she turns to him.
"I heard Joan Sutherland sing," she says.
"She wore a black and silver dress.
Sixty years old and she sang like an angel."
Then they dive to the black water below,

not knowing when it will hit, the way
the past hits, even with your arms
stretched out for re-entry.

Somehow

the rest of the mouse
fell through and the small skull
caught. It seemed to be chinning
itself on death from the wrought
iron grid of the garden table,
the place where we celebrate evening
by the wildly blooming camellia.
Beneath the table's grate the corpse
was suspended, tail a wan shoelace.
I put a small flowerpot
over the head and with paper towels
felt underneath for the body
which, like beauty, all but collapsed
in my hand. With a slight pull
it came away, leaving, under
the pot, the tiny too-big head.
There was no one to do this for me.
With the long blink we give
reality, I closed my eyes
and felt for the head
with paper, that instrument
of distance we allow ourselves
to burn or bury. It is enough
to live with the hand's perfect memory.

Chickens

In the killing yard a man sharpens
a razor, says a few words to God
and does a nice killing. After
plucking and gutting he cooks
the bird in a coat of its own
beaten eggs. When he eats the flesh
it is with pleasure. Every night
he goes to bed satisfied. Every day
he wakes up hungry. In heaven

the chickens complain and a chicken
angel is sent to earth. As the man
sleeps the angel helps him to dream
about red meat. No one suggests
the chicken should save the lives
of cows. Even in heaven angels
look out for their own kind.

The man wakes up with an appetite
for steak. He finds a cow
in a meadow but is intimidated
by its stare, the importance of
its dung. The man goes hungry.

All night the chicken angel sits
on the man's pillow and lectures
him about vegetables. By morning
the chicken yard is in the possession
of birds that cluck with authority
rather than resignation. Word
is out. They have an ambassador.

Instead of killing, the man decides
to cook the broccoli and potatoes
he finds on the table. But they
offer his teeth little resistance.
Vegetables, he decides, are
for children. Is it a wonder
the chicken angel asks himself,

"Have I been assigned to instruct
a stupid man?" As a last resort
the angel tells the man about
hunger, how it makes the body
clean and holy. The man is surprised
by the notion of fasting. He takes
the idea to a rabbi where it gets
a warm reception.

"Mazel tov," says the chicken angel.
It isn't his job to be sarcastic.

He heads for heaven having won
for chickens only a brief respite,
not that they expected more.

Zambia. Zimbabwe. On the Border

At the base of Victoria Falls the corpse
of a black woman lies. Kept fresh by mist
she has lain there more than a month
and is now leached perfectly white.
Even her hair. Maybe her eyes.
During this time she reflected light
in paler and paler colors to those who looked
down. It is said she found her sky
whole but her land torn—one country
ripped from the good earth of another.
Where the ground comes apart a mile-
long rift offers up paradise in a garden
asunder. She must have just stepped
over the knee-high barrier of thorns.

The Brain on Its Own

It was the brain's idea to leave
the body. Finally it could forget
the conundrum of marriage, the need
to be close and the need to be separate.
It would jet to Paris, maybe shop
for an outrageous thesis. But without
the body it could only dream of pleasure—
the brain was denied the special dispensations
of sex. Weather ceased to be an event.
How it longed for the hair's experiments.
The brain was bored. Given another
chance, it would squander every thought
on the flesh. It sought out the body,
serene in a bubble bath. The body
was stiff having danced all night
without feeling self-conscious.
And it was in love with another body.

A Surfeit of Desire

Your unerring sense of direction
has always hurried us through
what Merwin calls the anniversaries
of our deaths. You take
the linear route and I follow
describing my loop-de-loops.

Now with bodies shrunk from age
our appetites effervesce
with too much desire; we feel
we must travel farther, exercise
harder, love, love. Wait,
I'm coming. Soon enough we'll remain
in stasis. For the rest of our days
let's take all the time
in the world.
            Like stars
throwing off matter and fated
to collapse, our last destination
is inward. That being a bearing
I know how to take, dear heart,
you must let me go first.

Wings

Why are the children careless with their wings?
They have thrown them on the bed again
like coats of guests. These wings look light
but actually they're not, and just as it is

work for the children to fly, it is work
for us to pile their means of escape
in the fireplace, set them alight. Routinely,
we burn the gifts we've given them.
See how the protective glaze flares up

and is consumed while the armature blisters
like painted coat hanger wire. Next time
they want to fly, the children will wish
they had borne the weight. One day they'll be

able to throw out parts of their lives like us
deliberately, with no remorse—smoke a cigarette,
entertain a little death wish. My father once
put out a fire in my hair with his bare hands

never to touch me again.

Promise

My friend is dying
and knows it, not in the same way
the rest of us are dying,
but more exactly. I sat
with this friend and time passed
like scenery from the window
of a slow train. He referred
to a promise I'd made him.
What promise? I could not
remember. Neither could I
say, "What promise?"

Swimming

An old story—a man loved a woman,
wanted to please. When the Guernsey's
udder was stretched tight as a honeydew,
he milked. It was he who weeded
the trumpet vine out of the well
so the water tasted pure as the first
river. He could make the woman purr
when he gave her dipsy and skelter, but
it was not enough. "What will satisfy me?"
the woman wondered aloud. "If you were
a saint I should probably want a rascal."
Not that they didn't know satisfaction.
When they lay by the pond, she eased
his trousers to expose the place
where the tail had been, the shallow
white hollow above the cleft
of his buttocks. Now, for a moment,
I am content, she thought as she fondled
him there. It was as though she floated
over deep water without knowing
how to swim. "Tell me," she said,
"what kind of animal you were
when you had a tail and how you came
to lose it." "I do not remember,"
said the man. "Well, make something up,"
said the woman. "Were you the devil?"
The man closed his eyes in exasperation.
It was true the hair over his forehead
raised up in horns. Since he had been
old enough to comb he had tried

to smooth it. "Woman," he said, "how
can I please you?" "I want to love you
without reservation." As she said it,
she recognized that she had finally spoken
the truth. With her fingernail she traced
the boundary of his mysterious depression.
"All right," the man said. "I admit it.
I am the devil." "The devil would never
admit it," the woman said. "Truth
is strange," said the man. This man
could be the devil, thought the woman.
Is that why I love him? Is that
why I don't? "Perhaps my tongue
is your tail," she said. The man rolled
over, narrowly missing a cow pie.
As he did so, her hand fell away from its place
on his back and lay on the grass,
fingers curved in the way
of an opening fist or, as the man saw it,
a closing flower.

Odd

Suppose you'd never seen a bird
and came upon a one-winged duck.
The strange appendage dangles awkwardly,
appears to disarrange its side.
Where the side without a wing
is neatly feathered over, it looks right.

Advice

Daughter, do not clean the planet
for the astronomer who ignores
your breast to toy with stars.

Defy the lion tamer who asks you
to polish the chair he carries
to ward off beasts, offers you

unplucked dove to eat, a pony to curry.
Do not close your eyes when you listen
to music. The violinist wants you

to iron the linen under his chin.
Do not wait up all night
for a silent man to speak.

Find the one who carries
a dustpan. Look for
the janitor who knows his soap.

Entertaining Edelman; Ignoring Freud

Edelman returns with violets from his yard,
good bread and excellent wine he bought

in a serendipitous moment instead of the four bars
of soap Freud sent him for. Ignoring Freud,

who's in a pique, we pull up lounges on the grass
and Edelman expounds. The brain, alone, he says,

can deal with novelty. Edelman believes the brain
evolves, adapts what works, embeds us in the world,

the world in us. Across the lawn on an iron bench
Freud goes on and on while Grandmother hears him out

on penises and mother-lust. I rescue her, introduce
Edelman, prop his violets in a cold cream jar

reminding Grandmother she gave me cherry jam
in a similar one. Back then I expected the taste

of cold cream mixed with fruit and threw it out.
My fingers graze her pale old arm. Grandmother

shakes her head. That Edelman! From the borders
of our great calm white irises rise. Freud

relents, walks toward us. He's curious.

Going So Far

Goodbye, my darlings,
I'm trading our past
for a one-way
ticket to a far place
and I'm only still
here to throw out
letters you never received
with first lines so smart
they could not be followed.
The room, ankle deep
in what I have
pared from my heart,
will soon be tidy.
I am taking no paper,
no pen. No money.
One change
of clothes dyed
the color of mud.
I am ready to study
with lions, eat
meat enough
to make myself mean.

From

Inventory

(2008)

Where the Blue Begins

While I was walking down U Street
my daughter-in-law was making
a grandchild. I was walking
briskly so as to prolong my life, singing
Stairway to the Stars while the baby
was getting organized. Would it be
smart and dark and stubborn? Would it be loving
or rebellious? I was tossing and turning;
the baby was growing little arms and legs.
I was struggling with why are we here
while it faced up to the color of eyes.
It was a tadpole; I was a ferris wheel.
It was a snowfall and then I made a wish.
Three nectarines sat in a blue saucer.
Nearby, a piece of apple and seven raisins
soaked in gin. I was cooking supper
when I thought the baby turned its head,
pulled on the cord the way you do
when you want attention. I felt strongly
that it entertained a thought.
What? I said. What?

The Day of Death

It may be night. Don't worry,
the stars will come but they'll be
late. The moon will unwrap
the good silver. And all the planets
will be at their telescopes.

If you want silence,
you shall have it. If you want
talk you will finally
be heard. Even believed.

The autumn rain will fix
a yellow leaf to your shade
or winter cold will set
a crystal dish of snow

on the sill. There will be
no calling cards in it;
you won't have to meet
anyone new. You'll already
know everyone you love.

Channel Island Trail

The trail looms over a drop
to blue and a blood vine creeps
the chalky rock. What a long way

up we've come, resting a bit, then
pushing on, you from a colicky
babe to mom and me,

girl to geezer, a stitch in my side.
It's a dizzying height. The day is clean
and an ocean breeze pierces

the heat. Hand in hand
we perspire; not tethered
we're dry. Was it minutes ago

I untangled your hair,
bound up your knee.
And then you painted

a perfect world, forest
untouched except by sun,
the sea a plummet

too deep. This is as close
as you get to it,
the bloody industry of the heart.
The trail drops off so steep
from here. Turn around,
I am old. Help me down.

The Peach of Immortality

Born in winter under the tree
and abandoned to live, I was startled
by blossoms. Out of the box
of sky, petals fell like flakes
of cloud. Without any warning

hard fruits formed. I sat
in the shade and leaned in idleness
against the day. Vines sprang up
to fasten me, more powerful
even than gravity. As if

it were meant, the perfect sphere
of always fell in the hammock
of my lap without a bruise on it.
I caressed its fuzz with my thumb.
One bite, I knew, and I would live

three thousand years. If I ate
the whole peach I would live
forever. But I wasn't hungry.
I didn't love you yet.

Surprise Is Dying

I see my granddaughter caught
in a photograph, happy in a blue dress.
Blue. I could have guessed.
The moon rises and sets, rises and sets.
Look in my eyes. Surprise is dying.

Although I know the words to a hundred
songs, they're not today's songs.
Not tomorrow's. Singing has come
and gone. Running has slowed
to a walk. Laughter, dimmed to a smile.

Thinking, also, says pardon me
but I am sick of this. Reason
looks out at the world like a slow
gray fish in a small bowl. Books
prefer to lie closed on the shelves.

Old thoughts scratch behind my ear:
water the orange tree, make
the bed, where are my slippers?
Eating, though, continues to give
satisfaction. A date-nut cake. A rice

dish with curry and cinnamon.
Chicken baked in a very hot oven.
I taste a second helping of crisp skin,
dip a biscuit in my wine. And after
eating, I sleep. Sleep. I never tire of it.

Quantum Stuff

If we measure love's symptom
as passion, passion
is how it behaves.
If we measure its constancy,
constancy is the name
of the answer. The more exactly
we measure one thing
the harder it is
to measure the other.

Not even love's weight
can be counted.
Its system will change
in every process
and although the aftershock
of a kiss can expand
to many times
its original force
sometimes it doesn't.

The speed, the size,
the pleasure of it
cannot be separated out.
Nor any other aspect.

Love is the soul's
only perfection and has
every attribute.

About the Author

Elaine Magarrell (1928-2014) was born in Clinton, Iowa, and came of age there during World War II. Her father owned a ladies' ready-to-wear dress shop where the whole family helped out. She was educated at the University of Iowa and Drake University. She and her husband Jack raised their family in Des Moines and Iowa City. Although she wrote poetry from the age of ten, she burned her early work and did not write again until she was in her 40s and teaching English in a public junior high school. In 1981, she quit her job as a library clerk in the Washington Bureau of the *New York Times* to write full-time. She published in *Yankee*, *Passager*, *Poet Lore* and elsewhere. She is the author of a chapbook, *Inventory*, and two prize-winning books of poetry: *Blameless Lives*, recipient of the Washington Prize, and *On Hogback Mountain*, recipient of Washington Writers' Publishing House Prize. Her honors include numerous grants from the D.C. Commission on the Arts and Humanities and a Fellowship to the Virginia Center for the Creative Arts. She lived in Washington, D.C.

About the Artist

Debra (Magarrell) Conklin, an artist living and working in Los Angeles, is the daughter of Jack and Elaine Magarrell, both writers. She graduated from the University of Iowa with BA, MA, and MFA degrees in painting and education. She taught art to students from kindergarten to high school in Iowa, Minnesota, Massachusetts, and Los Angeles.

About the Editors

Barbara Goldberg

Barbara Goldberg, poet, translator, and editor, has authored five prize-winning books of poetry, including *Kingdom of Speculation* and *The Royal Baker's Daughter*. She and Israeli poet Moshe Dor translated his book of poems, *Scorched by the Sun*, as well as four anthologies of contemporary Israeli poetry. Goldberg is Series Editor of The Word Works International Editions.

Catherine Harnett

Catherine Harnett is a poet and fiction writer from Northern Virginia. She has authored two books of poems, *Still Life* and *Evidence*, and her poems, essays, and fiction have appeared in a number of magazines and anthologies, including the *Hudson Review*. Catherine has also translated poetry from Hebrew, and these are part of American and Israeli collections.

Jean Nordhaus

Jean Nordhaus' volumes of poetry include *Memos from the Broken World*, *Innocence*, and *The Porcelain Apes of Moses Mendelssohn*. In the past, she has served as poetry coordinator at the Folger Shakespeare Library and president of Washington Writers' Publishing House. She is current Review Editor of *Poet Lore*, the oldest continuously published poetry magazine in the U.S.

Other Word Works Books

Annik Adey-Babinski, *Okay Cool No Smoking Love Pony*
Karren L. Alenier, *Wandering on the Outside*
Karren L. Alenier, ed., *Whose Woods These Are*
Christopher Bursk, ed., *Cool Fire*
Barbara Goldberg, *Berta Broadfoot and Pepin the Short*
Frannie Lindsay, *If Mercy*
Elaine Magarrell, *The Madness of Chefs*
Marilyn McCabe, *Glass Factory*
Ann Pelletier, *Letter That Never*
Ayaz Pirani, *Happy You Are Here*
W.T. Pfefferle, *My Coolest Shirt*
Jacklyn Potter, Dwaine Rieves, Gary Stein, eds.,
    Cabin Fever: Poets at Joaquin Miller's Cabin
Robert Sargent, *Aspects of a Southern Story*
    & *A Woman from Memphis*
Fritz Ward, *Tsunami Diorama*
Amber West, *Hen & God*
Nancy White, ed., *Word for Word*

The Tenth Gate Prize

Jennifer Barber, *Works on Paper*, 2015
Roger Sedarat, *Haji as Puppet*, 2016
Lisa Sewell, *Impossible Object*, 2014

The Washington Prize

Nathalie Anderson, *Following Fred Astaire*, 1998
Michael Atkinson, *One Hundred Children Waiting for a Train*, 2001
Molly Bashaw, *The Whole Field Still Moving Inside It*, 2013
Carrie Bennett, *biography of water*, 2004
Peter Blair, *Last Heat*, 1999
John Bradley, *Love-in-Idleness: The Poetry of Roberto Zingarello*, 1995, 2nd edition 2014
Christopher Bursk, *The Way Water Rubs Stone*, 1988
Richard Carr, *Ace*, 2008
Jamison Crabtree, *Rel[AM]ent*, 2014
Jessica Cuello, *Hunt*, 2016
B. K. Fischer, *St. Rage's Vault*, 2012
Linda Lee Harper, *Toward Desire*, 1995
Ann Rae Jonas, *A Diamond Is Hard But Not Tough*, 1997
Frannie Lindsay, *Mayweed*, 2009
Richard Lyons, *Fleur Carnivore*, 2005
Elaine Magarrell, *Blameless Lives*, 1991
Fred Marchant, *Tipping Point*, 1993, 2nd edition 2013
Ron Mohring, *Survivable World*, 2003
Barbara Moore, *Farewell to the Body*, 1990
Brad Richard, *Motion Studies*, 2010
Jay Rogoff, *The Cutoff*, 1994
Prartho Sereno, *Call from Paris*, 2007, 2nd edition 2013
Enid Shomer, *Stalking the Florida Panther*, 1987
John Surowiecki, *The Hat City After Men Stopped Wearing Hats*, 2006
Miles Waggener, *Phoenix Suites*, 2002
Charlotte Warren, *Gandhi's Lap*, 2000
Mike White, *How to Make a Bird with Two Hands*, 2011
Nancy White, *Sun, Moon, Salt*, 1992, 2nd edition 2010
George Young, *Spinoza's Mouse*, 1996

The Hilary Tham Capital Collection

Nathalie Anderson, *Stain*
Mel Belin, *Flesh That Was Chrysalis*
Carrie Bennett, *The Land Is a Painted Thing*
Doris Brody, *Judging the Distance*
Sarah Browning, *Whiskey in the Garden of Eden*
Grace Cavalieri, *Pinecrest Rest Haven*
Cheryl Clarke, *By My Precise Haircut*
Christopher Conlon, *Gilbert and Garbo in Love*
    & *Mary Falls: Requiem for Mrs. Surratt*
Donna Denizé, *Broken like Job*
W. Perry Epes, *Nothing Happened*
David Eye, *Seed*
Bernadette Geyer, *The Scabbard of Her Throat*
Barbara G. S. Hagerty, *Twinzilla*
James Hopkins, *Eight Pale Women*
Brandon Johnson, *Love's Skin*
Marilyn McCabe, *Perpetual Motion*
Judith McCombs, *The Habit of Fire*
James McEwen, *Snake Country*
Miles David Moore, *The Bears of Paris*
    & *Rollercoaster*
Kathi Morrison-Taylor, *By the Nest*
Tera Vale Ragan, *Reading the Ground*
Michael Shaffner, *The Good Opinion of Squirrels*
Maria Terrone, *The Bodies We Were Loaned*
Hilary Tham, *Bad Names for Women*
    & *Counting*
Barbara Louise Ungar, *Charlotte Brontë, You Ruined My Life*
    & *Immortal Medusa*
Jonathan Vaile, *Blue Cowboy*
Rosemary Winslow, *Green Bodies*
Michele Wolf, *Immersion*
Joe Zealberg, *Covalence*

International Editions

Kajal Ahmad (Alana Marie Levinson-LaBrosse, Mewan Nahro Said Sofi, and Darya Abdul-Karim Ali Najin, trans., with Barbara Goldberg), *Handful of Salt*
Keyne Cheshire (trans.), *Murder at Jagged Rock: A Tragedy by Sophocles*
Jean Cocteau (Mary-Sherman Willis, trans.), *Grace Notes*
Yoko Danno & James C. Hopkins, *The Blue Door*
Moshe Dor, Barbara Goldberg, Giora Leshem, eds., *The Stones Remember: Native Israeli Poets*
Moshe Dor (Barbara Goldberg, trans.), *Scorched by the Sun*
Lee Sang (Myong-Hee Kim, trans.), *Crow's Eye View: The Infamy of Lee Sang, Korean Poet*
Vladimir Levchev (Henry Taylor, trans.), *Black Book of the Endangered Species*

www.ingramcontent.com/pod-product-compliance
Lightning Source LLC
Chambersburg PA
CBHW031632160426

43196CB00006B/381